artifacts

drawings + text
by

frank echenhofer

a flamingseed liminal book

drawings + text copyright © 2023
by frank echenhofer. all rights reserved.

ISBN 978-0-9892605-9-6

relaxing in the unknown chapbook series
a flamingseed liminal book / flamingseed.com

The seat of the soul is where
the human & non-human meet

I dream I am with a group of people
my group
I am not a leader but an equal

There is an
impending catastrophic event
about to occur

It's a natural event but it is unclear
if it's an earthquake or storm
or whatever

We are discussing
where best to go to survive

We are looking
for the best place to find
shelter

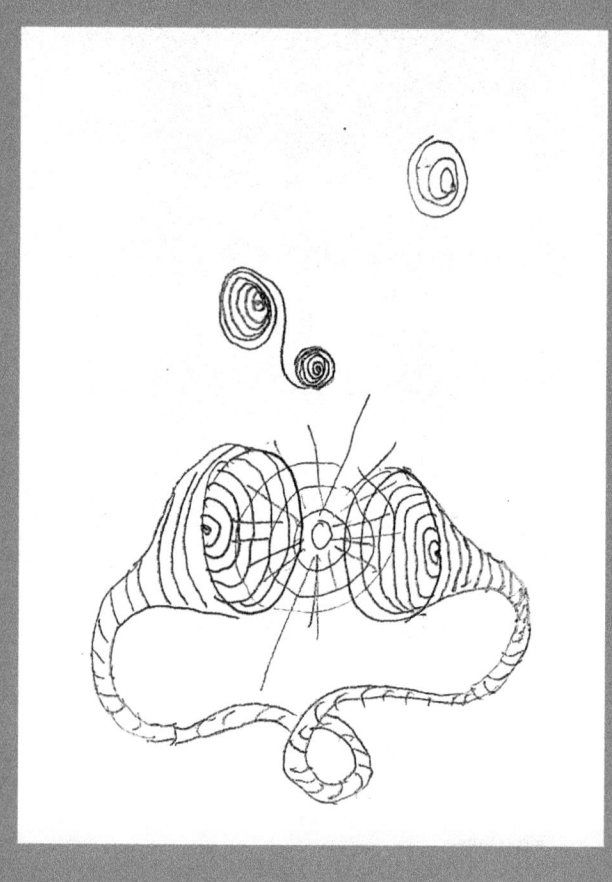

Let us look at
the dynamics
of the structure
of suffering

The sea grass
washes
to the left and to
the right in a tidal
pool

A crab hides upon a
narrow-cut ledge in the
sandstone
Sits facing the sea
carefully picking through
bits of things

A lifting claw approaches
an opening mouth

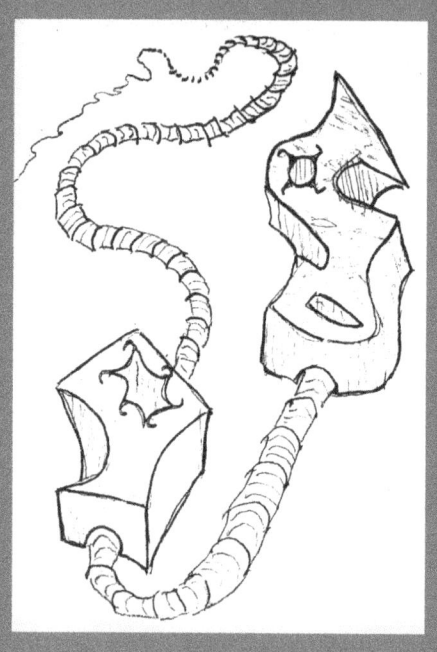

A gets advice
from an inner
guide (The "head")

A is instructed
to develop
relationships to
matter (4 elements
fear & desire)

A speaks to a
gentle feminine
entity

A has a run-in
with a violent
sexual female

The Vessel

The vessel contains
the process

It is a framework
for projection

Elements of experience
must have a structure
to have meaning
(content – form)

As growth occurs
fragments become
too restrictive & must
be split apart

When the projection is
withdrawn from the
body

When the projection is
withdrawn from the
relationship

When the projection is
withdrawn from the
ego

When the projection is
withdrawn from
matter

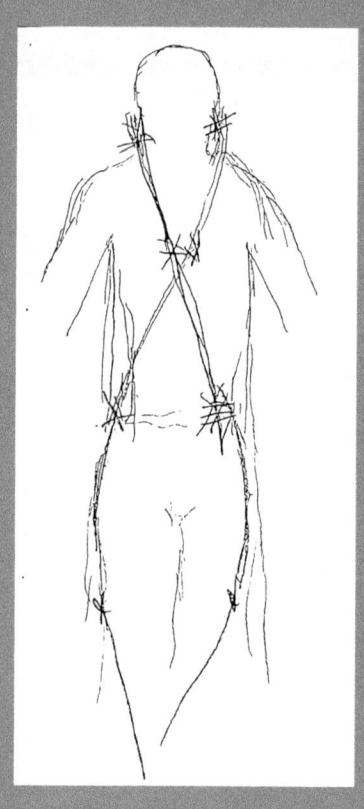

I dread seeing this
fearful result

Sadness seems a result
of the dread

Perhaps the dread
weakens me &
what I then feel is sad

Sadness for the
dream lost
the vision dashed
the hope withdrawn

It is so hard to find
a substantial base
from which to begin
At first
All is sheer bluff

When my thoughts push
too hard toward grasping
onto the nature of things

I forget
I am playing with
blocks in my mind
& mistake my
constructions for
something else

Belief is so mighty

It must be
for having lost it

For in many ways
I am weak
and restless

A very unique mood has
overcome me
One which
I have experienced
only several times before

There is a sadness and softness
that makes me quiet yet
not at all negative or
pessimistic

I am in awe of the sweet
delicate and fragile beauty
that characterizes
my existence

I am seldom roaring
with laughter
yet rarely do I howl in pain

The gentle and soft feelings
are my home
The gentle and delicate
beings are my friends

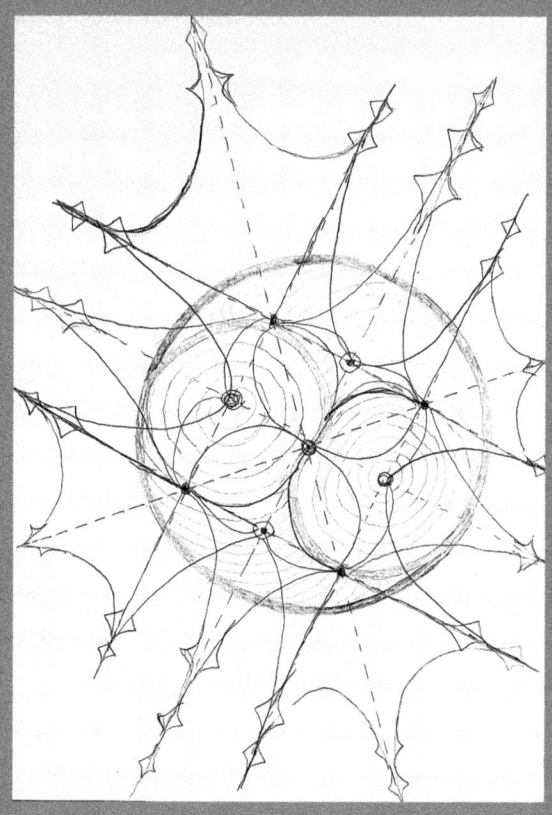

Suddenly all things are the
receptacles for my love
and for my devotion
yet at a distance I
find myself
not able or free to look on
lovingly without shame

All things seen and felt
in their fullness & vitality
have all my organs raped
and left my body washed
tired and alive

It was some time ago
that I lost my desire to know
the inner world workings
as a watchmaker knows his watch

Instead I have come to love
time filled and flooded
by events, carrying me
carrying me
mysteriously, mysteriously

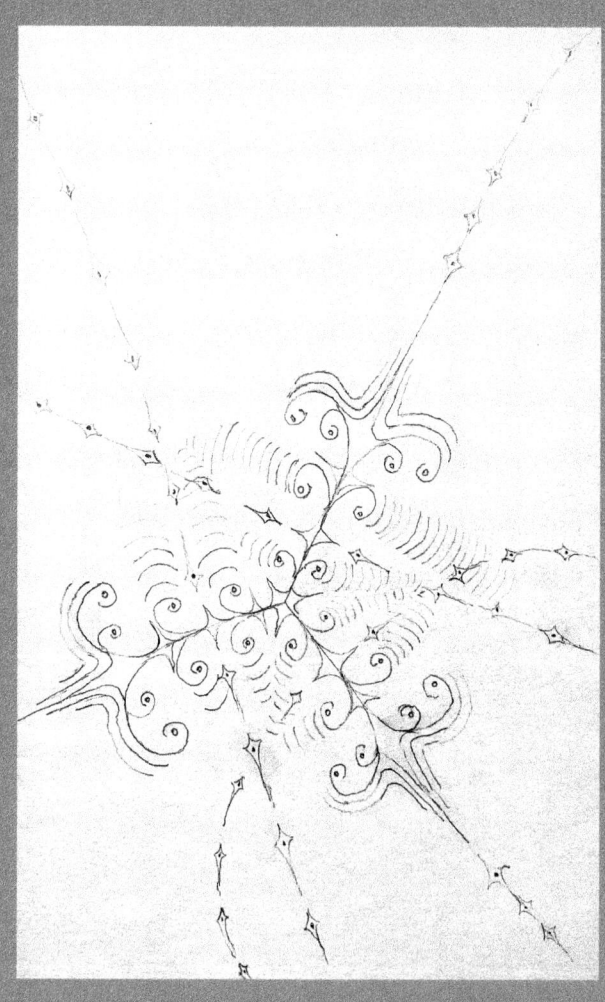

What my thoughts struggle with
my heart has always known
I have forgotten & recalled
& lost & found &
shunned and now again
To know is to feel

Bonds and ties are
shared always
What relief when they become partners
known and not spoken of
foolishly, unknowingly

Eyes meeting gracefully and directly
animal recognition
love overcoming fear
compassion and oneness
overriding mind, body, myself, yourself

What remains?

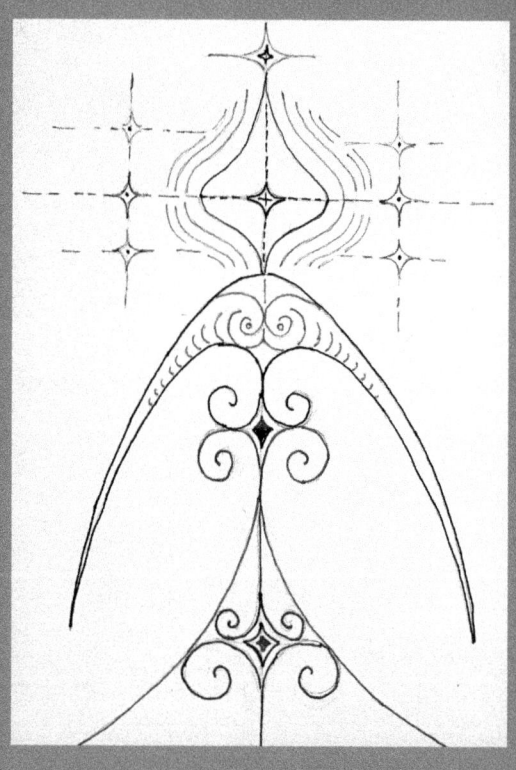

We all are no more
or less significant than
lightning striking
splitting limbs
from trees

Quiet now and whispers only
within at last
the free wild isolation
craving open-mouthed
and earnest

No time for
talking companions

Give me mutes
be they trees, open
spaces, heavy breathing

All are equally pure
and unlimited
as no word
ever mouthed

At last nothing is
important

I am glad not to
be obliged to smile
but instead look
blankly at the wall

I can glance casually
and curiously at
my reflection and
at what I touch
my intersection
with all else

What a wonderful and
bland miracle

The world is basically
content to be itself
moves not an inch
for no man
has no ears or heart
but is alive

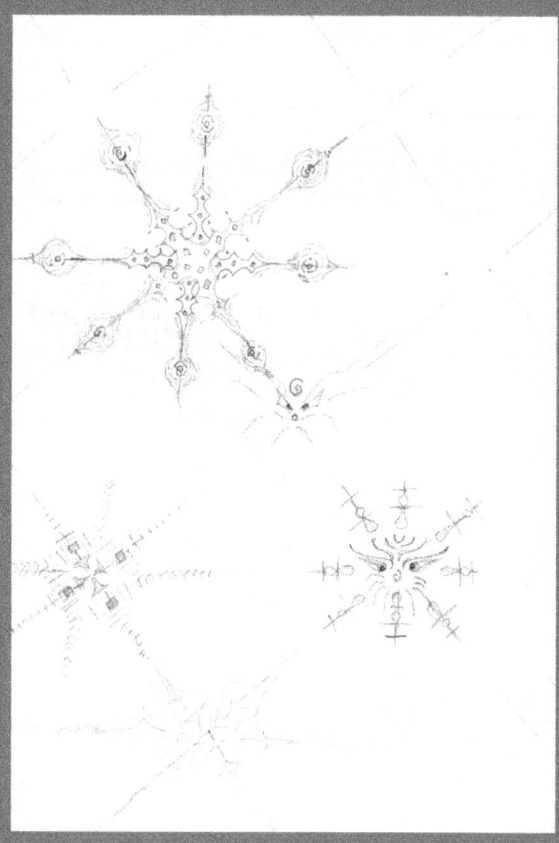

I imagine all the time
that a hypothetical
listener or being
has partial existence
in many people

There are glimmers
of recognition
in some eyes

I see that we two
will again someday be
together after eons
& eons of separated
vast space
worlds apart

I wish you would do
me the kindness of
stopping whatever
important things you
do or don't do
and make contact
with me

For I have been ready
for a visit for a while
now

It is not that I am
especially deserving
but I am
extremely curious
to know a few
basic things

Archive

The seat of the soul
is where the human
& non-human meet.

I am with a group of people, my group, I am not a leader but an equal. There is an impending catastrophic event about to occur. It's a natural event but it is unclear if its an earthquake or storm or whatever. We are discussing where best to go to survive. In the dream we are looking for the best place to find shelter.

Let us look at
the dynamics
of the structure
of suffering.

the sea grass
washes ~~with a~~
to the left and to
the right in ~~the~~ a tidal
pool~~s~~

~~The~~ a crab~~s~~ hides upon a
narrow cut ledge in the
sandstone.
~~It~~ ~~They~~ sits facing the sea
carefully picking ~~up~~ then
~~for~~ bits of things. ~~in to it~~
~~to it~~. A lifting claw approaches
an ~~to it is~~ opening mouth.

①

A~~A~~ gets advice
from an inner
guide ("The Head")

He is instructed
to develop
relationships to
matter (4 elements,
Fear + Desire,

A speaks to a
gentle feminine
entity.

A has a run-in
with a violent
sexual female

The Vessel

- the vessel contains the process

- it is a framework for projection

- elements of experience must have a structure to have meaning. (content – form)

- as growth occurs frameworks become too restrictive & must be split apart

My thinking

There are probably stages in the process whereby the process goes thru;

(1) when the projection is withdrawn from the body;
(2) when the projection is withdrawn from the relationship
(3) when the projection is withdrawn from the ego.
(4) when the projection is withdrawn from matter.

I dread seeing this
fearful result,
Sadness seems a result of
the dread, perhaps
the dread weakens me &
what I then feel is
sad. Sadness for the
dream lost, the vision
dashed, the hope
withdrawn.

P19

— way things
~~used~~ to be —

FANTASY
   MAY BE
~~whatever~~
   when~~ever~~
      no one will agree

It is so hard to find
a substantial base
~~from~~ which to begin.
~~For~~ At the first, all
is sheer bluff.

Exorcise "perhaps"

Let me loose or let
me give

When my thoughts push
to hard toward grasping
onto the nature of
things & forget that
I am playing with
blocks in my mind
& mistake my
constructions for
something else.

Belief is so mighty
it must be
for having lost it
in many ways
I am weak
and restless.

- A very unique mood has overcome me, one which I have experienced only several times before.

- There is a sadness and softness that makes me quiet yet not at all negative or pessimistic. I am in awe of the sweet, delicate, and fragile beauty that characterizes my existence.

- I am seldom roaring with laughter, yet rarely do I howl in pain

- The gentle and soft feelings are ~~those tha~~ my home,
- The gentle and delicate beings are my friends

Suddenly all things are the
receptacles for my love
and for my devotion
yet At a distance I
find myself
not able or free to look on
lovingly without shame.

All things seen and felt
In their fullness & vitality
have all my organs raped
and left ~~body~~ my
    washed, fried, and alive.

It was some time ago
that I lost my desire to know
the inner world workings
as a watchmaker knows
his watch.
Instead, I have come to love
time filled and flooded
by events, carrying me
~~But~~ carrying me
mysteriously, mysteriously

What my thoughts struggle with
my heart has always known
I have forgotten & recalled
and lost & found and
shuned and now,
again, to know is to feel.

Bonds and ties ~~will~~ are
shared ~~always~~
what relief when they
~~become~~ by partners
known and
not talked of
 foolishly, unknowingly;
Eyes meeting gracefully
and directly
 animal recognition,
love overcoming fear,
compassion and
~~needing~~ oneness over
riding ~~needs~~.
mind, body, myself, yourself
what remains?

We all are no more or less significant than lightning striking, ~~squirrels jumping from limb to~~ and splitting limbs from trees

The chance collection of ~~gaseous~~ molecules in a plotted portion of space

Quiet now and wispers only
within at last a~~ sound~~
~~the collective~~
~~Man~~ ~~Isolation~~ ~~of~~
the free wild isolation
craving open mouthed
and ernest
No time for ~~for companions~~
talking companions
~~Sit~~
Give me mutes
be they trees, open
spaces, heavy breathing
All are equally pure
and unlimited as
no word ever ~~was~~
mouthed.

At last, nothing is important

I am glad not to be obliged to smile but instead look blankly at the wall.

I can glance casually and curiously at my reflection and at what I touch, my intersection with <u>all else</u>.

What a wonderful and bland miracle.

The world is basicly content to be itself, moves not an inch for no man, has to ears or heart but is alive.

I imagine all the time that a hypothetical list'ner or being has partial existence in many people. There are glimmers of recognition in some eyes that I see that we two will again someday be together after eons of eons of seperated vast space far worlds apart.

I wish you would do me the kindness of stopping whatever important things you do or don't do and make contact with me for I have been ready for a visit for a while now. It is not that I am especially deserving but I am extremely curious to know a few basic things.

Afterword

This little book has been a delight for me to work on and publish. There is no way I could have done it without the loving and clear advice from my dear Jane Brunette—a real spiritual teacher of so many things, including how to find and express one's deeper voice.

It started with an exercise that Jane told me about. She had developed it for one of her writing groups to overcome a block that many people feel around their writing. In fact, many different kinds of blocks, but for me, after years in academia, it was finding my voice. It was crucial to think what that means—*my* voice—and it was through this process that I've reflected on all the many things I've written and never shown to anyone, all the efforts I've made that I've been too ambivalent to share. Through this process I've been able, with Jane's guidance, to find a voice within myself that I don't own, that is maybe a secret and truer part of myself. It has been an outstandingly beautiful and liberating process, and it might be of use to a few others to say a little bit about what that process was for me.

Jane mentioned that we've all written many things—all the people in her groups and perhaps you, too. We have notebooks and journals filled with things we've written that we've never looked at again, never fully reexamined, having the thought, I guess, that they were incomplete and weren't worth revisiting. My process involved locating notebooks and sketchbooks of drawings from my past filled with things I wrote down that I thought at the time were quite important, but had just stored away.

I was fortunate to have saved so many things. I collected them in a pile and slowly looked through them. I found things I had totally forgotten I had ever written that seemed fresh, as though from another person I was familiar with but who I didn't completely identify with. I've changed over the years, and to hear my own voice from the past was quite startling and interesting. On occasion, some of the voices felt strange, but on other occasions, there was something compelling I had really seen and I felt a thank you to myself for writing it down. Those are the things I pulled out and saved for this little book.

The process almost felt like a kind of archaeological dig. I was excavating my own buried past, dusting it off, looking at it again fresh. And what did I see? I loved some of it and some of it made me cringe. Some of it made me laugh, some of it made me feel a deep compassion for myself.

So that's what this little book is: a collection of artifacts, beginning with things I drew based on visions I've had, and on dreams. Some of the visions came from the use of sacred medicines. Some were spontaneous visions that came to me. Some of the drawings started as doodles and evolved into things I didn't even know were coming through me.

I chose the images first and set them aside, then looked through text that I had written. There were passages I found that spoke to me with a resonance that said they were meant to be pulled from the past and united with something in this present moment. And that's how this book came about: by commingling these drawings that activated something in me anew, expressing something I felt deeply and still feel deeply in myself, and the words that described similar things.

When I put the words with the images something new happened—something emerged that was larger than the words, larger than the images, because the two spoke to each other and a third thing arose that I'd never seen or felt before. This third thing was not an excavation, not an artifact, but something of this present moment.

I could have ended my small book at this point, but all of the text that accompanied my drawings had been handwritten, which in these days of keyboards, seemed archaic. Why not include photos of my journal pages themselves? A bit more material to make meaning with, perhaps, just as an archaeologist might include fragments of parchment with ancient script. For these reasons, I included the last Archive section.

All I can say is try this yourself or something like it, or discard it as a fool's errand, but I have to say for me, it was a sweet, beautiful process that I plan to continue. This little book will be followed by more books, perhaps similar in kind, taking things further. It is the beginning of something that is moving, that wants to come out and be shared with others.

So more to come.

—Frank Echenhofer
October 2023

About the author

Frank Echenhofer is professor emeritus at the California Institute of Integral Studies in San Francisco, specializing in spiritual psychology. He has done research in India with the Dalai Lama's most advanced meditators, and research with shamans in Brazil and Peru examining the benefits of ayahuasca and huachuma. In his private practice, he mentors individuals who wish to deepen their spiritual journey, drawing on the core teachings of the wisdom traditions in clear, concise and contemporary ways, assisting them to find reliable inner guidance for their own unique spiritual path. His website is frankechenhofer.com.